EUROPA ✠ MILITARIA Nº.

THE GREEN BERETS
Weapons & Equipment

Hans Halberstadt

The Crowood Press

First published in 1999 by
The Crowood Press Ltd
Ramsbury, Marlborough, Wiltshire SN8 2HR

British Library Cataloguing-in-Publication Data
A catalogue record for this book is available
from the British Library

ISBN 1 86126 300 7

Edited by Martin Windrow
Designed by Frank Ainscough/Compendium
Cover design by Tony Stocks/Compendium
Printed and bound by Craft Print Pte Ltd

Dedication:
For Chris Johnston, who knows something about soldiering.

Acknowledgements:
Many thanks, as usual, to those tolerant veterans of the late, lamented 12th Special Forces Group (Airborne), who shared their stories, insights, Airborne operations, trips to distant lands, and MREs, tequila, roast pig, and salsa with me. In the first rank of this assembly, for this current mission, I must credit former Command Sergeant Major Russell Mann, Captain (and Team Leader) Steve Trolan, SFC Buck Ravenscroft, and SFC Rick Cardin. Additionally, two accomplished Special Forces veterans of the Vietnam era - Lonnie Holmes and Dennis Mack - deserve a sincere salute. They provided many insights into how things really work when you are far, far from home and the bad guys are in the wire.

Steve Galloway at Heckler & Koch very kindly provided excellent images and information on H&K's superb weapons; SSG Mike Jacquard was generous with his time, and photographs; and David Wemhoff, another former 12th SF Groupie, helped considerably with the commo section. Sincere thanks to the whole assembly.

Reading and Research:
Steve Sherman is the clearing house for information about specific individuals who were assigned to special operations forces in South-East Asia, and he has developed an excellent database on people and units. Steve requests copies of orders to any Special Forces activity in the theatre; contact him at (713) 683-9076 and by e-mail to *sherman1@flash.net*. If you are looking for an old teammate or buddy, Steve's the place to start.

Steve also reprinted the Green Beret magazines published originally by 5th Special Forces Group in the late 1960s. These offer very interesting, often amusing insights into a very different time and place. Several other titles of special interest to former SF soldiers are also available from: RADIX, attn. Steve Sherman, 2314 Cheshire Lane, Houston, Texas 77018.

Author and editor also acknowledge their debt to the published research of Gordon L.Rottman, another 5th SFGA veteran, particularly his *US Army Special Forces 1952-84*, Elite Series No.4, Osprey Publishing (1985); *Armies of the Gulf War*, Elite Series No.45 (1993); and 'Anatomy of a Special Forces Camp' in *Military Illustrated* Nos.9 & 10 (1987 & 1988). Any errors are ours.

Contents

Introduction

Dozens of excellent books describe aspects of the legend and lore of US Army Special Forces. Some things have changed in the recent past – new weapons, new missions, new tools of the trade. At the same time, SF soldiers are careful to remember the many lessons learned from the past. This slender volume is a report on some of those lessons learned, particularly the ones relating to weapons and equipment. It is not intended to be a complete inventory of the SF armoury – that would take an encyclopedia, because SF uses almost any weapon, vehicle, radio, or tool (military or civilian) available in any nation around the world.

Army Special Forces is special in many ways. You can't really appreciate how the gear gets used without understanding a bit about the missions for which it is intended, or the doctrine behind the missions, so I have included a little about that. I have also included a bit about SF training, too. The missions, training, and tools of the trade are all intertwined – a mix of new and old, high-tech systems and blunt instruments, with a layer of tradition underpinning it all.

SF has been around long enough now that the first generation of professionals have just reached the end of their military career. Men like Russ Mann (see pages 49 and 63), with extensive combat experience since the Vietnam War and a full career in Special Forces, have now retired. With the departure of these veterans goes a great store of military wisdom, survival skills that can't be learned in a peacetime environment. So this seems the right time for a brief look at the tools and tricks of the Special Forces trade, new and old - an introduction to the best of the past and the present.

Sgt. Lonnie Holmes, a Special Forces medic, on patrol in Vietnam. He wears the 'tigerstripe' camouflage clothing designed and manufactured by the legendary Ben Baker's support operation on Okinawa. (Photo Lonnie Holmes)

*   *   *

My first introduction to the US Army's Special Forces came in a little Montagnard village way out in the backwoods of central South Vietnam, some time in the fall of 1962. We had flown in with our CH-21C Shawnee helicopter from 8th Transportation Company out of Qui Non, to deliver ammunition and supplies to an A-team working with the local tribesmen out in the middle of enemy territory. The Viet Cong had been operating in the area for years, abusing and exploiting the tribesmen without any interference from the South Vietnamese government - who themselves despised and maltreated the hill tribes.

After dumping the crates and sacks and ammo boxes, I had a chance to prowl around the village. It made an intensely exotic impression. The houses were all elevated off the ground on stilts, and were made of poles covered with thatch. Pigs, children, and an occasional baby elephant wandered around the area. The women wore only handsome hand-woven skirts, brass necklaces, and big smiles.

Further exploration discovered the men of the village. Under the command of one of their own, they were doing close-order drill right there in the dusty village street. They were attired in loincloths, simple shirts, and nothing more. Each carried a weapon of some sort – old American M1 carbines and .45cal 'grease guns', German MP.40 9mm submachine-guns - all World War II surplus.

Supervising the proceedings were a couple of lanky Green Berets. They watched the drill with a critical but approving eye. As well they should – because these tiny tribesmen, with their bare feet, loincloths, and antique weapons, were in perfect step. There was something gleeful about them – a kind of pride that comes with a new skill and new opportunities – which made a profound impression on me at the time.

I didn't entirely understand it at the time, but I do today: those few American soldiers, with their unconventional mission and headgear, were accomplishing a kind of military magic. They made it possible for these little Stone Age tribesmen to defend themselves effectively, for the first time in centuries of abuse by the lowlanders. With a little help from SF, these highland tribesmen began making life unpleasant for the Viet Cong passing through their home hills. The Green Berets were the catalyst for a reaction that essentially beat the Viet Cong in the Central Highlands during the next few years - the golden age of Special Forces. It didn't last, but not because of any failure by the Green Berets or their allies.

About 20,000 men of the United States Army Special Forces served in South-East Asia from the late 1950s through the early 1970s, in Vietnam, Thailand and Laos. Of these, 640 were killed in action, 134 were missing in action, six died of wounds outside the theatre of operations, and 26 were killed accidentally. Seventeen Green Berets received the Medal of Honor for actions in South-Eeast Asia - more than any other individual command in the war.

3

Special Forces Missions

The Special Forces, popularly known around the world as 'the Green Berets', are just one of several US Army organizations tasked with the most challenging missions. Apart from the highly visible paratroopers and airborne units of US XVIII Airborne Corps, who do the 'heavy lifting' when overseas force projection is required, these groups include the superb light infantry battalions of the 75th Ranger Regiment; the 160th Special Operations Aviation Regiment; and various Psychological Ops, Civil Affairs, and Special Ops Signal and Support units.

These forces, along with the units of the US Air Force Special Operations Command and the US Navy's Special Warfare Command, are each specially trained and equipped to execute specific and very hazardous operations with a minimum of support and with maximum speed. All these organizations are under the command and control of a joint headquarters, US Special Operations Command - USSOCOM; the Army elements' chain of command passes through US Army Special Operations Command (Abn) - USASOC - at Ft.Bragg, North Carolina.

The mission of the Green Berets, however, is special even within this select community. Rangers, paratroopers, and the USAF Special Ops Wings typically execute conventional missions with unconventional speed, shock, and surprise; but they do so in uniform, using conventional tactics and standard-issue weapons. Green Berets train for missions that require the

tact, cultural understanding, and language skills of a diplomat. The core of their task is to work with the indigenous population, wherever they are sent; as well as being superbly skilled soldiers, they are trained to be teachers, leaders, and evangelists. These missions sometimes involve assignments where no triggers are pulled, where nobody is killed or injured. Yet Green Berets are also tasked with assignments requiring extreme violence: very small SF units are trained to wreak tremendous havoc among enemy conventional and unconventional forces.

This combination of warrior and diplomatic skills makes for interesting people and missions, and SF have more than their share of both. Although you don't read much about them in the papers any more, they are still out there - helping out, teaching, and spreading the doctrine - sometimes in rather nasty places. Their principal missions today fall under these main categories:

Unconventional Warfare

The historical models for UW were the Operational Groups and 'Jedburgh' teams organized by the Office of Strategic Services and its Allied counterparts during World War II. These extremely daring men (and a few women) were inserted, often by parachute, into occupied France, the Low Countries, Italy, Greece, Yugoslavia, China and South-East Asia, bringing with them radios, small arms, and leadership ability. They recruited, trained, organized, and supervised delivery of equipment to groups of local partisans, and sometimes led them in attacks on Axis forces. During the Vietnam War the UW mission seldom required parachute insertion, but it included all these other skills during operations deep in enemy-dominated territory.

Direct Action

This mission tasks an SF unit with an overt or covert action against an enemy objective. It might involve an attack on an isolated command facility, the demolition of a bridge, dam, powerhouse, headquarters, or aircraft. Direct action missions also include prisoner-snatches and rescues, ambushes, raids and mine-laying operations. An important mission in recent years has been insertion deep within enemy territory with Laser Target Designators, to 'illuminate' targets for stand-off or direct attack by aircraft or artillery using precision munitions.

Special Reconnaissance

These missions task SF units to gather information for theatre commanders, often by infiltration deep within hostile territory. SR missions require collection of all kinds of information – on terrain, populace, military and civilian activity – that may be useful for conventional or special operations forces. SF recon teams provide surveillance of targets before and after attacks.

Foreign Internal Defense (FID)

These missions employ the SF soldier's teaching and language skills to help train soldiers in friendly nations around the world.

In addition, SF units are tasked with **Counter-Terrorism (CT), Psychological Ops (PsyOps), Civil Affairs (CA), Coalition Warfare/Support, and Humanitarian and Civic Action (HCA)** missions.

(Left) East Africa, c.1984: Chris 'Jersey' Scheurman, medical NCO, Operational Detachment A-591, 5th SFGA, in the Kenyan bush somewhere near Narok. He wears the US Army's 'plain vanilla' Olive Green 107 fatigues, sterile - i.e. bearing no identifying markings or insignia. (Photo Mike Jacquard)

(Below) Central America, 1986: 7th SFGA personnel provide basic training for local troops in handling US weapons, movement techniques, ambushes and assaults at a time when regional guerrilla warfare threatened to spill over the borders of several vulnerable states.

(Opposite) FID has been an important, if undramatic mission for SF during the past 20 years, providing some of the challenges of the UW mission without the hazards of behind-the-lines wartime operations.

Organization

The organization of Special Forces units has been shaped from the beginning by their core mission: to insert small teams of very highy skilled specialists into territory threatened by the enemy, to assemble, train, arrange the supplying of, co-ordinate, and if necessary lead in action indigenous guerrilla groups. This mission was formulated in 1951 by Brig.Gen.Robert A.McClure, chief of the US Army Psychological Warfare Section, who formed a small planning staff of World War II veterans of such operations in Europe and the Far East.

Against considerable resistance from Army officers wedded to more traditional concepts, and from the CIA - who wanted to control this type of operation themselves - Gen.McClure won the support of Army Chief of Staff Gen.J.Lawton Collins, and of President Eisenhower. On 20 June 1952 the first unit, the 10th Special Forces Group (Airborne), was activated at Fort Bragg, NC, under command of Col.Aaron Bank. The type of recruits he sought were mature professionals with foreign language skills, willing to accept not only unusual risks but also responsibilities beyond their conventional ranks. Volunteers were soon responding, and included many World War II veterans of Ranger and Airborne units, Merrill's Marauders, OSS Operational Groups, and recent refugees from Communist countries. In 1953 the second unit, the 77th SFGA (later retitled 7th) was activated, and the 10th was shipped to West Germany.

The Special Forces Group

The key to Special Forces organization is the flexibility to tailor assets to fit a particular task. The initial Table of Organization and Equipment for 10th SFGA consisted of a Headquarters & Headquarters Company (HHC) which controlled a number of separate Special Forces Operational Detachments (SFODs) which had different functions and compositions. Rather than operating like conventional battalion or regimental teams, which have more or less permanently established unit strengths and 'wiring diagrams', SF were to deploy on operations the number and mix of SFODs suitable for that particular mission, 'plugging in' or omitting varying numbers and types of sub-units as required - what we would today call the 'modular' approach.

At each level the Detachments - usually termed D-, C-, B-, and A-Teams, in descending order - were remarkably small by conventional standards, made up of minimum numbers of officers and senior NCOs with unusual levels of individual skills. The minutiae of organization have changed to meet differing circumstances over the past 45 years, but the essential structure has survived.

While the Army uses the conventional 'company' and more recently 'battalion' in describing this structure, the reader should remember that in the SF context these terms do not mean the same as in line units. The mission of the SF Detachment is not to field large numbers of fighting infantry, but to provide an armature of specialists around which large indigenous forces can be formed.

Organization when in garrison is slightly different than when deployed; the B- and C-Teams are augmented by administrative and service elements so that they can function as more conventional company and battalion headquarters respectively. Army Reserve (11th, 12th) and National Guard (19th, 20th) SFGAs have at times had fewer assets than Regular units.

During the Vietnam era - the early 1960s to early 1970s - the basic organization of a Group was as follows. The SFGA was a colonel's command; when its detachments were deployed to a theatre of operations, he headed a single D-Team in-country. This staff had six officers and 18 NCOs. The Group's HHC provided command, control and service support for a varying

number of deployed detachments, and the Signal Company handled comms upwards, downwards and sideways. (Briefly, in 1963-65, the Group also had its own Aviation Company.)

Below the Group, three C-Teams (six officers and 12 NCOs, commanded by a lieutenant-colonel) each had regional command and control responsibilities. Each C-Team controlled from two to five district B-Teams (six officers and 17 NCOs, commanded by a major).

Each B-Team controlled between four and ten (or even more) A-Teams deployed to dispersed locations. This - on paper, with two or three officers and 11 or 12 NCOs, little more than a strong squad - was the heart and soul of SF operations.

The A-Team

The Special Forces Operational Detachment 'A' consisted (and consists) of 12 to 14 men trained to operate independently and effectively behind enemy lines for months at a time. The primary mission of the A-team during the Cold War was Unconventional Warfare. At one time it was thought that an A-Team could organize an indigenous force of up to 1,500; but although some teams in South-East Asia did control remarkably large groups, since then the figure of 500, or roughly a battalion, has been accepted as more realistic.

In the 1950s-1980s the A-Team had two officers: a captain team leader, and a lieutenant who functioned as executive officer - the latter has since been replaced by a warrant officer. A master sergeant served as operations sergeant, assisted by a sergeant first class who handled intelligence. There were two weapons sergeants, two engineers, two medics, and two communications NCOs. All the enlisted men were cross-trained to be qualified in one or more of the other specialties. All members of the team were supposed to be proficient in at least one foreign language spoken in the team's region of interest (although that requirement is not always met today). The A-Team can be split neatly in two, with an officer or warrant officer, team sergeant, commo man, medic, engineer, and weapons man in each, and still conduct effective operations.
(See diagrams below for current organization.)

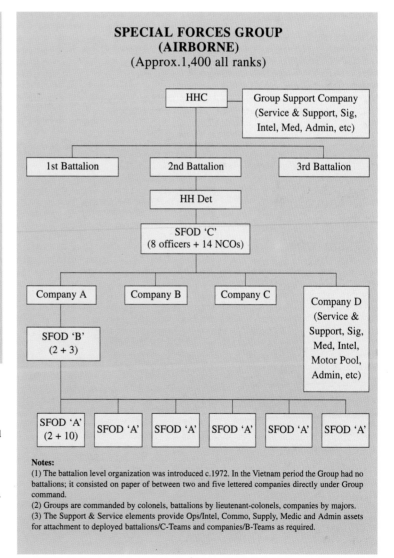

**SPECIAL FORCES
OPERATIONAL DETACHMENT 'A'**

Detachment Commander *(Captain)*
Executive Officer *(Warrant Officer)*
Operations Sergeant *(Master Sergeant)*
Intelligence/ Asst.Ops Sergeant *(Sergeant First Class)*
Senior Weapons NCO *(SFC or Staff Sergeant)*
Junior Weapons NCO *(SFC or SSGT)*
Medical Specialist *(SFC or SSGT)*
Assistant Medical Specialist *(SSGT or SGT)*
Radio Operator Supervisor *(SFC or SSGT)*
Chief Radio Operator *(SGT)*
SF Engineer Sergeant *(SGT)*
SF Engineer *(SGT or SPEC 5)*

Notes:
(1) The size of the A-Team has varied over the years between 6 and 15 officers and men; and exact NCO grades in the different slots also vary. Prior to the mid-1980s the team had two commissioned officers, the XO being a lieutenant.
(2) Exact composition has also varied depending upon theatre and mission; e.g., in Vietnam from late 1968 the 14-man A-Team had two Intelligence sergeants, only one Demo NCO, and a third officer assisted by a Spec 5 for Civic Action/Psychological Operations.
(3) Until the 1980s the Senior and Junior Weapons NCOs were termed Heavy and Light Weapons Leaders.

**SPECIAL FORCES GROUP
(AIRBORNE)**
(Approx.1,400 all ranks)

HHC — Group Support Company (Service & Support, Sig, Intel, Med, Admin, etc)

1st Battalion — 2nd Battalion — 3rd Battalion

HH Det

SFOD 'C' (8 officers + 14 NCOs)

Company A — Company B — Company C — Company D (Service & Support, Sig, Med, Intel, Motor Pool, Admin, etc)

SFOD 'B' (2 + 3)

SFOD 'A' (2 + 10) — SFOD 'A' — SFOD 'A' — SFOD 'A' — SFOD 'A' — SFOD 'A'

Notes:
(1) The battalion level organization was introduced c.1972. In the Vietnam period the Group had no battalions; it consisted on paper of between two and five lettered companies directly under Group command.
(2) Groups are commanded by colonels, battalions by lieutenant-colonels, companies by majors.
(3) The Support & Service elements provide Ops/Intel, Commo, Supply, Medic and Admin assets for attachment to deployed battalions/C-Teams and companies/B-Teams as required.

Opposite Three soldiers of the 7th SFGA pose in front of 'Bronze Bruce', the memorial at the Special Warfare Center, Fort Bragg, NC. The captain at left wears his rank bars through the 7th SFGA's red flash on his dark green beret; and Lightweight Battle Dress Uniform, with subdued cloth insignia including the Expert Infantryman Badge and jump wings. The NCO at right wears standard BDUs with the PASGT ('Fritz') helmet and basic load-bearing equipment.

The staff sergeant, centre, wears Army Green Class A uniform. Note Special Forces crest pinned through beret flash; jump wings, on teal blue and yellow background; Combat Infantryman Badge above medal ribbons; and three 'hash marks' marking nine years' completed service. (Photo William B.Folsom)

Basic Unit History

There is obviously no space in this book for a comprehensive history of the authorization, inactivation and deployments of all SF units since the 1950s, but the basic dates for the Regular SFGAs are as follows. Where a Group was given special responsibility for an area, it may be assumed that training and liaison teams were widely deployed to nations in that area thereafter.

1952   10th SFGA activated; divided to form 77th SFGA. Psychological Warfare Center & School (incorporating Special Forces School) established at Ft.Bragg, NC.

1953   10th SFGA posted to West Germany, with special responsibility for European operations.

1954-57   77th SFGA send training teams to Japan & SE Asia.

1957   1st SFGA activated on 77th SFGA cadre, with special responsibility for Asia; first teams deployed to Vietnam. PWC&S renamed Special Warfare Center & School.

1959-62   77th & 1st SFGA teams deploy to Laos.

1960   77th becomes 7th SFGA. 10th SFGA team deploy to rescue civilians in Congo.

1961   President Kennedy orders expansion of SF. 5th SFGA activated, for SE Asia operations. CIDG programmeme begun by US Army advisors in Vietnam. Team A-35, 1st SFGA, establish first SF camp.

1962   USASF Vietnam formed to control rotating teams from 1st, 5th & 7th SFGA.

1963   3rd SFGA (African responsibilities), 6th (Middle East) & 8th (Central & South America) activated.

1964   5th SFGA takes over Vietnam operations with HQ at Nha Trang.

1964-69   Massive expansion of 5th SFGA assets and missions.

1966   1st SFGA assets deploy to Thailand, remaining until 1974. Reserve 11th & 12th and National Guard 19th & 20th SFGAs consolidated from smaller units.

1969   3rd SFGA inactivated.

1971   5th SFGA returns to USA; reformed using assets of inactivated 6th SFGA. Small SF detachments remain in Vietnam and Cambodia until 1973.

1972   8th SFGA inactivated; 3rd Bn., 7th SFGA takes over Latin America responsibility.

1974   1st SFGA inactivated.

1977-78   5th SFGA form interim 'Blue Light' counter-terrorist unit.

1978   1st SFOD D ('Delta Force') activated for counter-terrorist operations, working directly under JSOC.

1980   Delta mount abortive Iran Embassy hostage rescue.

1982   1st Special Operations Command activated.

1983   Delta take part in Grenada invasion.

1984   1st SFGA re-activated.

1989   3rd SFGA re-activated.

1990-91   5th SFGA, with 7th, 3rd & 10th SFGA assets, deploy to Saudi Arabia; widespread operations in liberation of Kuwait.

Current Strength

At this writing, seven Special Forces groups are authorized:

Group	Home Station	Area of Specialized Interest
1st SF Group	Fort Lewis, Washington	Pacific and Eastern Asia
3rd SF Group	Fort Bragg, North Carolina	Caribbean and West Africa
5th SF Group	Fort Campbell, Kentucky	SW Asia and NE Africa
7th SF Group	Fort Bragg, North Carolina	Central and South America
10th SF Group	Fort Carson, Colorado	Europe and Western Asia
19th SF Group (ANG)	Camp Williams, Utah	Asia
20th SF Group (ANG)	Birmingham, Alabama	Europe and Western Asia

Note: The Army Reserve 11th & 12th SFGA were inactivated in the early 1990s, although the National Guard 19th & 20th SFGA were retained.

Vietnam

The 77th and 1st SFGAs sent training teams to work with South Vietnamese forces from 1957 - only three years after the French withdrawal and the partition of the country. What would become their major role emerged in 1961. Large areas of the Central Highlands and Mekong Delta were completely undeveloped, and occupied by ethnic, religious and political minority groups who had been neglected or maltreated by successive governments. Whichever side enlisted the wholehearted help of these marginalized groups could dominate large swathes of strategic terrain, which were ripe for exploitation by the elusive Viet Cong.

The Civilian Irregular Defense Groups set up in 1961-62 were employed, trained, clothed, fed, equipped and paid directly by the US Army. In accordance with their core mission, Special Forces A-Teams began setting up camps at Montagnard villages late in 1961, combining civic action (i.e. improving the neglected villagers' lives, and providing medical care) with military training and organization. By the next year the project could boast some 200 villages and 12,000 armed 'Yards'. With village defence in place, more aggressive 'strike' units were set up and led by SF personnel on surveillance and local security missions; by the end of 1963 there were 18,000 CIDG 'strikers' as well as 43,000 village militia, advised by two B-Teams and 22 A-Teams. By 1969 the CIDG counted well over 40,000 men in Camp and Mobile Strike Forces, trained and organized by some 2,300 Green Berets in eight B- and about 50 A-Teams.

(**Above & left**) SF on patrol in the Vietnamese Highlands; reconnaissance, surveillance and interdiction of known VC/NVA infiltration routes was a central task. (Photos Dennis Mack)

(**Opposite**) Early SF camps were fairly flimsy affairs, constructed of local timber and thatch with scrounged corrugated iron and crates. Protection depended on a trench and earth berm, not enough wire augmented with *punji* stakes, and a few sandbagged machine gun bunkers and mortar pits. On 6 July 1964 the camp at Nam Dong, Thua Thien province, run by Detachment A-726 from 7th SFGA, was attacked by Viet Cong in battalion strength. It held out largely through the courage of a dozen SF soldiers and 50 Nung mercenaries, and the luck of having an inner perimeter inherited from an old French post. Here the team leader, Capt.Roger H.Donlon - wounded four times that night, and awarded the Medal of Honor - returns in September to inspect the ruins. (US Army)

(Above & left) A-Team members lead CIDG irregulars on patrol. 'Tigerstripe' clothing of VN Marines and Rangers was acquired or copied locally, or ordered from third-country sources under the US-funded MDAP programme (Mutual Defense Assistance Pact); exact colour and design details varied widely. Two SF and one LLDB (ARVN Special Forces) personnel usually accompanied each patrol. The Americans are more heavily loaded than the 'strikers' (whose dark complexions suggest an ethnic Khmer unit); SF men provided all medical and communications support.

(Opposite top) An early stage of camp construction - dug-in cargo containers with timber overhead cover.

(Opposite bottom) Typical appearance inside a completed camp: note sandbag and oildrum bunkers, communication trenches, weapon pits, high wire, and cleared strip between camp and village. (Photos Dennis Mack)

(Above) External view of a 'hardened' or 'fighting' camp, typical of A-Team positions from the mid-1960s. The overrunning of a few camps (Hiep Hoa, November 1963; Polei Krom and Nam Dong, July 1964) led to an up-grading of camp defences. A typical garrison might be a CIDG Camp Strike Force of 300-400, in companies segregated by ethnic origin; an SF A-Team of three officers and 11 NCOs; and their counterpart ARVN Special Forces (LLDB) team - *officially* in command. An inner perimeter protected the essential positions - SF and LLDB team quarters, operations, ammo, generator, supply, commo and medical bunkers. This might be defended (as was, e.g., A-333's Chi Linh camp in Binh Long province) by 3 x 81mm and 1 x 4.2mm mortars, 6 x .30cal and 2 x .50cal MGs, and 3 x 57mm recoilless rifles. Outer perimeters had several belts of cattle and concertina wire seeded with trip-flares and Claymore anti-personnel mines; at Chi Linh 19 x .30cal MGs and 9 x 60mm mortars were emplaced in pits and bunkers, sometimes capped with concrete; and an ARVN artillery platoon of two 105mm howitzers might be assigned to the camp. Tough and loyal ethnic Chinese Nung mercenaries were often hired to stiffen the garrisons; and 'doorbell' forward positions were installed and manned some distance outside the main perimeters. (Photo Lonnie Holmes)

(Left) Spec.4 Dennis Mack fraternizing with a local. SF soldiers often forged much closer relationships with indigenous groups than men of conventional US units, since they lived and worked alongside them for many months at a time. Their good relations, contrasting with the mutual hostility between the Montagnards and other minorities and the LLDB teams co-located with SF A-Teams, often led to tension. Note full-colour insignia on Mack's OG 107 jungle fatigue uniform. (Photo Dennis Mack)

(**Right**) In camp SF members usually wore standard olive green jungle fatigues with full insignia. Those visible here are sergeant's chevrons; the Special Forces shoulder patch; the gold-on-black AIRBORNE tab above the patch; jump wings on his left chest, and on the left pocket the tiger's-head patch of the CIDG Camp Strike Forces.

On operations the 'tiger-stripes' were almost universal, with a matching 'boonie hat' with or without the brim cut down. Green Berets enjoyed a good deal of latitude in assembling the combat clothing and gear which suited them best. (Photo Lonnie Holmes)

(**Left**) When the opportunity offered, Special Forces soldiers were not averse to supplementing their rations with fresh fish. Favourite lures included hand grenades or small blocks of C4 plastic explosive, which proved quite effective. (Photo Andrew Dulina)

Camp Strike Force units comprised three or four 130-man companies plus a reconnaissance platoon and a civic action team. The camps were usually located in remote areas, where the CSF carried out local and border security, trail surveillance and general intelligence-gathering missions within a radius of perhaps 100-200 square kilometres. They were often quite successful in missions which took realistic account of their level of training, discipline and equipment.

Mike Forces

Mobile Strike ('Mike') Forces grew out of the CSF, due to the need for mobile reaction units to support threatened camps at short notice (US and ARVN conventional units were seldom available when needed). In July 1965 the C-Team assigned to each of the ARVN Corps Tactical Zones was authorized to raise a battalion-size MSF; a 5th MSF was also raised for country-wide operations controlled directly by 5th SFGA. Each Mike Force was commanded by an A-Team. In 1966 they were each enlarged to between two and five battalions, and in 1967 a B-Team was assigned to control each MSF. The 1st, 2nd and 5th MSFs were mostly recruited from Montagnards, the 3rd and 4th from Nungs and Khmers. Airborne-qualified, these units were trained and equipped for aggressive operations, and did well in many actions - including four airborne assaults during 1967-68.

An offshoot of the MSFs during 1966-67 were the Mobile Guerrilla Forces - one per CTZ - which each consisted of a CSF company plus a recce platoon led by a SF A-Team, without LLDB involvement. They carried out 'Blackjack' infiltrations, ambushes and raids in enemy territory, with great success. They continued these after absorbtion into the Mike Forces in late 1967.

MACV-SOG

Although a joint service organization, Military Assistance Command Vietnam - Special Operations Group contained many Special Forces soldiers. MACV-SOG was a joint unconventional warfare task force, set up in 1964 to conduct ultra-sensitive long-range reconnaissance and direct action missions inside North Vietnam, Laos and Cambodia. SF personnel assigned to MACV-SOG were among the last to leave Vietnam in 1973.

* * *

The year 1969 was the high water mark of Special Forces activity in Vietnam. 5th SFGA had five companies in-country. One was assigned to each ARVN CTZ - C (I CTZ), B (II CTZ), A (III CTZ), and D (IV CTZ). Each of these C-Teams controlled between two and four B-Teams, one controlling the Mike Force and each of the others running between eight and 14 A-Teams. Company E had eight B-Teams, and was responsible for special missions - long-range recce and intelligence-gathering, including cross-border operations. Given the very limited numbers of Green Berets in-theatre, their achievements were out of all proportion, and completely vindicated the Special Forces concept.

(**Opposite & above**) Strikers prepare their weapons and gear at Bong Son; and line up on the LZ to be airlifted into an operation in II CTZ. Note the blue scarves - colours provided quick unit recognition in the field. (Photos Lonnie Holmes)

(**Right**) A Montagnard CSF striker inspects a Viet Cong cache. He is armed with the M79 grenade-launcher or 'blooper', a characteristic squad weapon of the Vietnam War. The 40mm high explosive grenade had a maximum range of 350 metres, though local terrain often limited its use to less than a third of that distance. This soldier's clothing is locally made, and most of his web equipment is US issue; but the so-called 'indigenous' or ARVN rucksack was popular with American soldiers too, for its large capacity and comfortable suspension system. Note M18 smoke grenade carried on his web suspenders. (Photo Dennis Mack)

15

(**Opposite top**) Out in the open, with no cover or concealment, a patrol checks out a wet valley bottom in the coastal area of II CTZ. Shortly after this photo was taken, enemy on the hillsides opened fire; a counter-attack by the patrol produced three enemy KIA. (Photo Lonnie Holmes)

(**Opposite bottom**) In striking contrast, this photo taken during an operation in closely wooded terrain - with a carpet of dead leaves - underlines the extraordinarily difficult and dangerous conditions of jungle patrols, where an 'encounter battle' could flare up without warning at a couple of metres' range. (Photo Dennis Mack)

(**Above**) A team in deep undergrowth cover get on the horn - the PRC-77 radio. The fact that both are smoking suggests that there is no immediate risk of action. (Photo Lonnie Holmes)

(**Left**) A Viet Cong camp on fire after an artillery strike called in by a Special Forces patrol from a nearby firebase. (Photo Dennis Mack)

Foreign Internal Defense

The post-Vietnam era saw a rapid run-down in SF units and manpower. (This was not regarded as a disaster by some 'true believers', who felt that the huge mid-1960s expansion had encouraged a relaxation of individual standards.) Over the next decade SF kept a low profile; but they remained active overseas, sending teams to train the forces of several friendly countries, particularly in Latin America. These photos show SF personnel of 7th SFGA training local conscripts near San Pedro Sula, Honduras, in 1986-89, when that nation's borders were threatened by the overspill of guerrilla warfare from Nicaragua during the 'Contra' period and from El Salvador. Within a few weeks these boys will be conducting real combat patrols, and some will probably be killed or wounded. As well as teaching small unit tactics in the field, the SF provided instruction in clearing buildings.

The Gulf War

Each of the five regional unified commands into which US forces are divided has its own Special Operations Command to co-ordinate the special forces of the three services when deployed on joint operations. Early in the deployment of US Central Command forces to Saudi Arabia for Operation Desert Shield in August 1990, following the Iraqi invasion of Kuwait, US Special Operations Command Central transferred from its base at MacDill AFB, Florida, to Riyad. A considerable number of special units from the Army, Navy and Air Force were progressively deployed to form Joint Special Operations Task Force Central. During the preparation phase and the shooting war which followed in 1991 these units carried out a very wide range of missions.

The main SF unit deployed was 5th SFGA, reinforced by personnel from the 7th and 10th and the newly re-activated 3rd SFGA. When they first arrived in theatre the 5th SFGA were employed in training Coalition forces from Arab nations, and Kuwaiti refugees, in specialist skills. They were then attached in more than 100 liaison teams to Coalition contingents, providing navigation aids, intelligence, and links with air and artillery fire support assets.

In conjunction with the British SAS the SF units also mounted cross-border operations into Kuwait and Iraq even before the air war began (using, among other equipment, Russian-made Mi-8 helicopters). Inserted by air and by various vehicles - including the DMVS modification of the 'Humvee' -

SF teams carried out deep reconnaissance and surveillance, prisoner snatches, combat search and rescue (two companies of 10th SFGA), target designation, general intelligence-gathering missions and raids. They penetrated not just Kuwait City but even Baghdad itself. Delta Force carried out SCUD hunts in western Iraq. All in all, this was the largest Special Operations Forces deployment ever attempted by the USA; and it required all other SOF units to contribute special equipment items such as long-range radio gear, sniper rifles, and Laser Target Designators to bring the inventory of the deployed units up to war strength.

(Below) Dave Lange, a member of OD A-581 from B Co., 3rd Bn., 5th SFGA photographed at Wadi Al-Bateen, Saudi Arabia, in a 'Hummer' mounting a Mk19 40mm grenade-launcher. He wears DCU - Desert Camouflage Uniform - with a Detroit Tigers baseball cap. Battledress uniform was worn 'sterile', without insignia, except for the occasional addition of rank badges. (Photo Mike Jacquard)

(Opposite top) SF soldiers instruct officers and men of the Kuwaiti 2nd Inf.Bn., 15th

Brigade in the use of the M16, MAG-58 and RPG-7.

(Opposite bottom) Men of OD A-592 with a weapons cache found duirng building clearing operations in Kuwait City, 1991. Left to right: Kuwaiti Lt.Khalid, SFC Mulcahey, SSG Norris, SGT Cyr, SFC Bruner. All wear sterile DCU, with armour vests acquired locally; these had ceramic and steel plates, giving better protection for EOD work than the US Army's standard issue PASGT ballistic armour. (Photo Mike Jacquard)

Special Forces Training

From the beginning, Special Forces has been designed for special soldiers. In the 1950s it was restricted to older (although not always more mature) soldiers of sergeant rank or above, qualified as parachutists. Both those required qualifications slipped a bit during the mid-1960s when manpower was urgently required for the huge effort in Vietnam, but they are securely in place again today. There are four formal phases of instruction and testing in the 'Q-Course' at the SF School at Ft.Bragg before a man can qualify for Career Management Field (CMF) 18 and wear the green beret.

Phase One: Special Forces Assessment & Selection

The first is the selection and assessment phase, SFAS. This is a three-week ordeal which quickly filters out anybody who is not in perfect physical condition, by means of timed 'ruck' (rucksack) marches of 17 miles and more. You don't know how far you have to go, and you don't know how long you're allowed to get there – so you try to jog along with a 35-pound ruck on your back, and pray no blisters develop - bleeding feet are common. Less common are attempts to replace the heavy contents of the ruck with a pillow, but they do happen, and are grounds for immediate dismissal.

Candidates run the dreaded obstacle course regularly, float in the pool for hours, and wander the backwoods of Camp Mackall with map and compass, searching for well-hidden landmarks. The SFAS phase tests the individual's emotional maturity, intelligence, and social skills. You need to be able to work successfully with others; misfits quickly disappear. Instruction during SFAS includes land navigation, small unit tactics, rappelling, and some other basic skills; but this phase is planned more as an ordeal to be survived than an educational programme. For those who survive the three weeks, an assessment board meets to decide who gets to move on to Phase Two.

Phase Two: Individual Skills

If you make it through SFAS, the next phase provides individual skills. For enlisted soldiers that means one of four specialties – weapons, engineering, communications, or medical.

The weapons specialist has 24 weeks to become highly proficient with all US and most common foreign small arms. He gets to the standard where he can quickly field-strip each, re-assemble it, fire the weapon - and, crucially, teach someone else to do the same. He learns all about anti-armour weapons, current and obsolete, and how to improvise weapons from common materials. He can make a rocket-launcher from two pieces of wood and a battery, and knows how to prepare a booby trap. He knows how to call for artillery, how to use laser designators, plan fields of fire and fire control procedures, and how to emplace and employ anti-aircraft weapons. Instructors test his small arms expertise with the dreaded 'Pile Test' – five weapons, completely disassembled (not field stripped), in one big pile of parts. The student has 30 minutes to put all five back in working order.

The engineer specialist programme also lasts 24 weeks. The candidate learns about building field fortifications, bridging techniques, construction techniques for buildings and canals. He learns a lot about explosives – C4 in blocks and ribbons, TNT, det cord, prepared cratering charges, and improvised explosives and munitions.

SF medics study for over a year before completing their training. When they are done, they are more skilled in trauma management than most doctors. They can perform many kinds of surgery, administer antibiotics and controlled pain medications, carry out many kinds of dental procedures, set fractured bones, and are expert at stitching up wounds – on animals as well as people. They are qualified to function not merely as skilled combat medics, but as the only clinician within many miles' reach of an isolated and perhaps primitive civilian community.

Commo specialist training lasts 37 weeks. Students become

(**Opposite top**) All SF soldiers are required to be Airborne-qualified; a three-week course at Ft.Benning features a lot of running and PT.

(**Above**) Students on the Q-Course are expected to record progressively better performances during the programme - an added stress in an already stressful environment.

(**Right**) The cargo net is a standard feature of the course, with which the student will become intimately familiar.

proficient in Morse code, radio procedures, and operation of many US and foreign radio systems. There is a lot of emphasis on burst transmission and satellite communications, both very important technologies in current SF operations. The course concludes with an around-the-world communications exercise.

Phase Three: Collective Training

Attrition during the first two phases of instruction is quite high, often filtering our well over 50 per cent. Survivors go on to the final formal phase of the Q-Course - Collective Training, and the dreaded 'Robin Sage' exercise. Now the individual soldiers are assembled as an A-detachment, complete with commander, XO, two medics, two commo men, a pair of engineers, and two weapons specialists. They are assigned a mission, placed in isolation, and then parachuted at night into North Carolina's Uwharrie National Forrest.

They land in the mythical nation of Pineland, a country peopled with suspicious local residents who might or might not co-operate, might or might not betray the team. The students set up drop zones, assemble guerrilla units, and conduct operations against 'hostile' forces, using all the skills learned during Phases One and Two.

Only after successfully completing all three phases of the Q-Course is a man qualified to wear the beret. Then the real training begins, in his unit, to continue for his entire career.

(Right) Phase I is supposed, among other things, to test 'confidence and motivation', but endurance and obstacle courses continue throughout the programme. Once this student has struggled to the top of the Grinder he will have to walk along an elevated beam about 12 feet in the air; a mis-step will result in a painful fall and probable injury.

(Below) Rapelling from Camp Mackall's tower intimidates some students.

(Above) If you can't go over an obstacle you may have to go under it - like everything else, the low crawl beneath barbed wire has to be performed at speed and without hesitation.

(Right) If there's no way over or under, then the only way left is 'through'.

(**Opposite top**) When you emerge from this hole you have to get yourself out of it without touching the yellow lines.

(**Opposite bottom**) Training never stops throughout a Green Beret's career. Here men from OD A-591 do a little refresher on techniques for rapelling down a mountain with a casualty strapped in a stretcher. Note the distinctive shape of the 'cat's-eye' reflector worn on the back of the cap by the team medic at right, Michael 'Doc' Thomas. (Photo Mike Jacquard)

(**Above**) SSG Dennis Mack makes his presentation during a 'brief-back' before a mission. These students have just endured a five-day phase without food while all training continued.

(**Right**) Mission planning is meticulous, including study of terrain models.

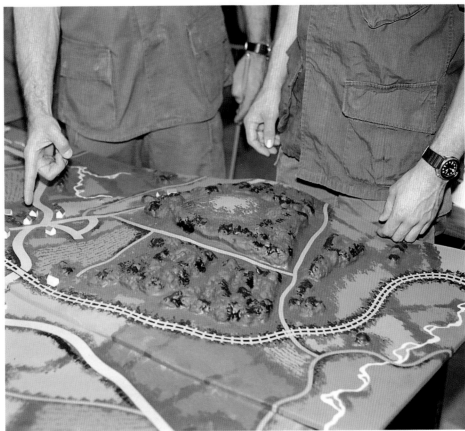

Weapons

'The Special Forces soldier has to be familiar with numerous weapons systems because, as a special operator, you use weapons as tools, and you need different tools for different jobs. There are times, for example, when you will need to carry the enemy's weapons – to give you the same silhouette, and the same sound signature when you fire.

'A lesson learned in Vietnam: you want to have everybody on the team firing the same weapon, if possible. There were times in Vietnam when some guy would be carrying a Swedish K [9mm Carl Gustav M45/b sub-machine gun], another a CAR-15, and somebody else an AK. In the heat of combat sometimes these guys would start shooting at each other, based on the sounds of the weapons. And you can't trade magazines, either, if you're using different weapons. Of course, there are always exceptions to this rule, based on the mission; but in general you try to keep the team equipped with the same weapon system.' (SSG Buck Ravenscroft)

Over the years Green Berets have used just about every weapon available for real-world missions. That includes .22cal pistols with improvised suppressors, cut-down Russian RVD machine guns, and antique sub-machine guns like the .45cal M3A1 'grease-gun' from World War II.

In fact, all Green Berets must be proficient with dozens of foreign and obsolete weapons, and with good reason – you need

(Above) For the enthusiastic shooter, a mouth-watering range of firearms are available for this training session at Ft.Bragg. Unfortunately, if you shoot them, you have to clean them... Just a few of the types identifiable in this stack are the 'Swedish K', Israeli Uzi, Russian PPSh-41 and Beretta M19 sub-machine guns; Browning Automatic Rifle and M2 .50cal, FN-MAG 58, M1919A6 .30cal and Russian PK machine guns; M1 Garand, M14, G3, AKMS and Moisin-Nagant rifles and M2 carbine. In the background is an old Russian wheeled carriage for a heavy MG or an RCL. (Photo Mike Jacquard)

to be able to use whatever is available locally, anywhere in the world. That often means Russian, German, British, French or Italian weapons, or very elderly American models, issued to soldiers in Africa, Asia, or South America. World War II vintage small arms were often very ruggedly built, and if they have been looked after lovingly they are still lethal. Not only must a Green Beret understand how a foreign weapon is used, he has to be able to instruct others how to use it effectively - and to perform the instruction in a foreign language.

However, the primary weapons for most SF soldiers are the same ones issued to conventional combat and combat-support units: the M16 rifle, M60 and M249 machineguns, and M9 Beretta pistol. In addition, though, SF units are frequently issued specialized and unusual weapons like the excellent new SOCOM .45cal pistol, the Barrett .50cal sniper rifle, and the compact carbine version of the M16, the Model 723. What follows is a brief run-down on some of the more common weapons in the SF armoury.

(Left) The A-Team heavy weapons man naturally has to be completely familiar with standard squad machine gun types such as the US M60 ...

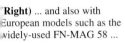

(Right) ... and also with European models such as the widely-used FN-MAG 58 ...

(Left) ... and the more recent Heckler & Koch Model 21.

(Above) Current standard issue 5.56mm M16A2 rifle, here with off-set scope sight mounted.

(Below) SF soldier firing the M16A2. He wears the old OG 107 fatigues, basic belt-order load-bearing equipment, and a 'drive-on rag' made from a triangular bandage in place of a cap.

The M16 'black rifle' has been general issue for nearly 40 years now, and is likely to remain so for many years to come. It weighs just under 8lbs, takes 30-round magazines, and has a theoretical accurate range of 800 metres - about half a mile; under battle conditions it is rated effective at 400 metres. It was the first general-issue infantry weapon to embody the then-new concept of a small calibre round - 5.56mm is equivalent to .233in - propelled by a powerful charge, giving a flat trajectory and

equivalent accuracy and stopping-power to one of the heavier World War II generation rifles.

The original model introduced during the 1960s suffered the teething problems which are inevitable when a new system is issued to a conscript army in the middle of a war, especially on an Asian battlefield. Much aluminum was employed in its manufacture, and the smaller, lighter construction

of most parts compared to the old .30-06 War II M1 Garand and the M14 demanded more careful cleaning and maintenance. A change of ammunition propellant also complicated matters. The A2 has a chromed chamber, heavier barrel, reshaped forestock, hard plastic (replacing fibre-glass) butt and pistol-grip, and other detail refinements which make it an accurate, reliable and effective infantry weapon.

One of the most significant improvements offered by the A2 is the 'controlled burst' feature. The initial model had three settings: safe, single shots, and fully automatic. In combat this often encouraged inexperienced soldiers to choose full auto, and they quickly depleted their ammunition supply by the tactic known as 'spray and pray'. The A2 change lever has settings for safe, single shots, and a three-round burst. Even so, only your first round is likely to be a bull's-eye, because the muzzle will still elevate during delivery of the burst; but in battle its firepower advantage outweighs this theoretical drawback.

(Above) M16A2 with integral M203 pump-action 40mm grenade-launcher. Conventionally this weapon - introduced at the end of the 1960s and still standard issue - is carried by at least one man in every four.

The launcher fires HE, multiple projectile (i.e. canister) and parachute flare rounds, and has a range of 350 metres. The grenade arms itself within 14m to 27m of leaving the muzzle; the HE round's effective radius on detonation is about 25m, but it could cause injury within 130 metres of the detonation. In Vietnam it was noted that at very short range even an unarmed round did appalling damage if it hit an individual.

(Below) Detail of the M16A2 with grenade-launcher sights attached.

In Vietnam the experimental XM177E2 sub-machine gun was carried, a military version of the commercial CAR-15 - a short-barrelled M16 with a telescoping butt-stock. Essentially the same weapon is now designated as the M4 carbine. Only 31ins long, it is a light, comfortable weapon, easily carried on a parachute jump. Recoil is light, with minimal muzzle rise; the M4A1 variant offers full-auto fire. With its shorter sight radius and barrel the M4 is inherently less accurate than the rifle, but is an effective weapon for its intended missions - ambushes, 'meeting engagements' and close-quarter battle.

(Opposite top) SSG Rick Cardin armed with one of the three variants of CAR-15, with a 20-round magazine. Note that his rucksack - the large combat pack of the ALICE system - has been spray-painted with black blotches for camouflage effect, and he has inserted a foam rubber pad between his back and the frame. (Inset) The small size of the 5.56mm round allows each pouch of the ALICE system to hold three M16 magazines - 90 rounds. Special Forces often carry a considerably greater load than the infantryman's 180 rounds.

(Opposite bottom) Firing an early M4 carbine, with 30-round magazine.

(Right) Among the elderly foreign weapons with which SF personnel have to become entirely familiar are the Soviet-designed Kalashnikov AK47/AK74 assault rifle series - certainly the most widely distributed small arms in the world, with tens of millions in circulation throughout the former Communist bloc and the Third World.

The AK47 was much maligned by Western observers when it was first encountered in Vietnam - it was said to be a crude weapon with a weak cartridge and dubious accuracy. Combat experience changed a lot of minds. The AK is a simple, durable weapon, highly effective when used within 200 to 400 meters. Strange as it may sound, its major deficiency is probably its loud safety selector - the clicking of 20 or 30 of these switching from SAFE to FIRE all at once alerted many US units to NVA ambushes before a shot was fired.

(Below) The RPG7 shoulder-fired rocket grenade launcher is almost as common as the AK rifles. With a fixed battle sight and a telescopic sight, it is effective up to about 500m; at 900m the grenade self-destructs. It is launched by a propellant charge, and then boosted by a charge in the projectile; it can penetrate 320mm (12.6in) of armour, but is used world-wide as general purpose 'artillery' at squad level.

(Above & below) The AKMS is a folding-stock model of the Kalashnikov family, taking the same 7.62mm x 39mm 'short' round as the original AK47 assault rifle - slightly lightened and modified, with a stamped rather than a milled steel receiver, but essentially the same weapon. It weighs just under 9lbs, measures 34.25ins overall, and has a 16.34in barrel. The AKMS takes 30-round magazines, and fires single shots or fully automatic. The sights are graduated to 1,000m, but any target beyond 500 or so is pretty safe; firing single shots, you can achieve a six-inch group at 100 metres. It is cheaply made, but extremely tolerant of rough handling and battlefield dirt. It is employed all over Eastern Europe, Asia, Africa, the Middle East and South America in its tens of millions, and ammunition is therefore very widely available all over the world. Special Force teams have often made use of this series of weapons when circumstances demanded.

(Above) Winchester Model 1200 pump-action 12 gauge shotgun.

(Below) SSG Mike Jacquard with the Winchester 1200; such weapons are often carried by the point man on patrol. Since the Winchester M1987 of World War 1 the US Army and Marines have recognized the 'trench-sweeping' qualities of a fast-firing shotgun with heavy loads. Under war conditions various models - from Winchester, Mossberg, Remington, Ithaca, Savage, etc. - have been made available on a generous scale to assault troops. Their tubular integral magazines hold between three and five rounds, and 'magnum' loads are available.

These weapons come into their own in the 'meeting engagement' or first encounter at close quarters in heavy cover; and as 'contact breakers', when SF personnel need to buy a few moments' respite from close contact when withdrawing in a hurry. Under these circumstances precise marksmanship is impractical; the priority is to seize the initiative by filling the air with lead – a task for which a 12-gauge pump gun is ideally suited.

(**Above**) Of all the weapons on the battlefield, pistols probably kill the fewest people (second only to the bayonet, which is in practice more of a domestic tool). Even so, pistols remain a legitimate part of the Special Operations armoury. During the Vietnam era .22cal pistols were frequently used (with and without silencers) to incapacitate enemy soldiers without killing them when prisoners were needed. Typically, this involved a carefully placed shot to the right shoulder, preventing the enemy from using his weapon (as long as he was right-handed). The pistol was also, and still is, an instrument for killing people quietly at very close range. Since even the 9mm cartridge used in the standard-issue Beretta M9 pistol is unreliable for putting somebody down permanently, Special Forces now issue instead the **Mk23 pistol**, developed by Heckler & Koch for USSOCOM as the Offensive Weapon Handgun System.

Based on the tried-and-true

.45cal ACP cartridge used in the Army's beloved old M1911 Colt pistol, this new handgun features tremendous knock-down power, match accuracy, and modular attachments designed for the special needs of SOCOM shooters. The Mk23 is rather bulky, 1.5in thick and almost 10in long – with the optional sound suppressor, over 16 inches. With a standard ten-round magazine loaded with ball it weighs about 3.25 pounds. Trigger pull is somewhat stiff, at about 12lbs for the first (double-action) shot and about 5lbs for the remaining (single-action) rounds.

Instead of conventional lands-and-grooves the Mk23 barrel has polygonal rifling. It is remarkably accurate: during evaluation tests it averaged 1.4in five-shot groups at 25 metres using service ammunition, and averaged better than 6,000 rounds between stoppages. Unlike most match-grade handguns, the Mk23 is expected to perform to this standard after

immersion in water, mud, and body fluids. A high-temperature O-ring seals the muzzle/slide opening until the weapon cycles, helping to keep out grime. The muzzle is threaded to accept a sound suppressor. Such big-bore pistols are not usually silenced, but the Mk 23's is

pretty effective, reducing the sound signature to about 132 decibels - about as loud as a .22cal pistol. The front of the frame is grooved to accept accessories like a tactical flashlight or a laser pointer, both of which are designed specifically for the pistol.

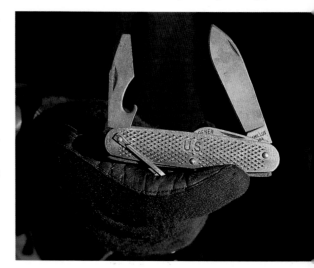

(**Right**) Smaller weapons such as his H&K 9mm P9 are also frequently carried as back-up or 'hide-out' weapons. Although soldiers tend to like them for reasons of folklore, most pistols have no value on the conventional infantry battlefield except as 'contact-breakers' at hand-to-hand range; consistently accurate shooting at even 10 metres' distance takes talent and a lot of regular practice. 'Choosing which pistol to carry is like choosing underwear - it's entirely a matter of what the individual is comfortable with' – SSG Mike Jacquard.

(**Left**) Most SF soldiers like knives and own a variety of them. They are essential tools of the trade, at least on patrol; their merits are debated and tested. Some carry massive blades the size of small swords, while others rely on much more modest versions. While these big knives are considered weapons by those who carry them, they are very seldom used that way. Only two Green Berets of my acquaintance have killed people with knives - one a sentry killed with a thrown blade, the other an NVA soldier surprised and stabbed in the chest during a messy dawn encounter in the enemy trenches outside Khe Sanh.

As Russ Mann says, 'Ninety-nine percent of what you do with a knife involves opening C-rations and slicing baloney. Your choice of knife, therefore, ought to be something that is very good for slicing baloney, that you could also use to stab somebody if it ever comes to that.'

Everybody, it seems, carries a Leatherman combination knife or one of its equivalents. These combo knives are really just elaborate and expensive versions of the old Boy Scout knife, with a variety of blades and tools for almost every occasion. (Of course, the old Boy Scout knife didn't have a dynamite cap crimper ...)

(**Opposite bottom**) Standard issue pocketknife as found in flyer's survival kits, and often carried by Special Forces.

(**Left**) This ancient blade belonged to a team leader's father, who used it in Vietnam.

A favourite close-quarter-battle weapon is the Heckler & Koch MP5 sub-machine gun; this is available in 9mm, .40 Smith & Wesson, and 10mm – the three standard pistol cartridges used by American military and law enforcement personnel. The Green Berets like it, firstly, because it is reliable; and secondly, for its ergonomics - it is easy to carry and operate. The shrouded sights prevent snags on clothing, the safety is 'ambidextrous', and the weapon manoeuvers easily and naturally when engaging targets. A selector permits single shots, three-round bursts, or full automatic. It is accurate within its intended range - normally, about 15m, and often much less. A 'silenced' version, the MP5SD, is sometimes used by SF teams. Thirty small holes near the muzzle bleed off some of the gas pressure behind the bullet, slowing it to sub-sonic; as the bullet emerges from the muzzle the suppressor slows down the release of propellant gasses, reducing the weapon's report to the point where the loudest sounds are the bolt recycling, and the bullets striking the target.

(Above & left) Among the most popular SF weapons is a very light (6lbs), compact version of the MP5, the MP5K (for *kurz*, 'short'). With a 6.8in barrel and a fore-end pistol grip, it is a tiny 32-shot machine pistol, easily concealed under a jacket, under a vehicle seat or in a glove box. SF troopers call the MP5K, with its cyclic rate of fire of 550rpm, the 'room broom' - it is used to sweep up clusters of enemy personnel, normally in enclosed spaces. Recoil is negligible and muzzle flip in full auto is very light. An SF soldier on an entry team equipped with an MP5 will be expected to make 100 per cent kills – no misses at all, and consistent head shots. Its effective range is listed as 200m, but with such a short barrel that is an unconvincing figure under any but the most perfect range conditions.

(Above) Snipers normally work in two-man teams, one man shooting while the other provides security and spots for him. They typically wear 'ghillie suits' of camo net and burlap strips, and pull their weapons and equipment behind them in a 'drag bag' as they squirm slowly towards their position. Snipers are often assigned missions where they don't fire a shot: their training makes them the ultimate observers. They can melt into the landscape and stay there for days at a time, reporting on enemy movement. But when appropriate, they can infiltrate to within a kilometer of a forward enemy airfield or vehicle park, killing personnel and disabling aircraft, trucks, and even APCs with single .50cal armour-piercing slugs though the engines and electronics bays.

(Left) View through the 10x scope on an M24 rifle at very close range - perhaps 100m. This is for a 'no reaction' shot - a head shot which will kill the target without him making any sound or movement.

39

Snipers

Americans got interested in long range sniping even before the Revolution. Precision marksmanship at long range has been part of our tradition since Colonial times, when putting food on the table and defending the family cabin might depend on an individual's skill with the long-barrelled flintlock rifles perfected in America by 18th century 'Pennsylvania Dutch' (actually German) gunsmiths. Marksmanship made a significant difference on some Revolutionary War battlefields, and there is documented evidence for occasional hits at up to 400 yards. During the Civil War special sniper rifles like the Whitworth were produced with heavy barrels, hexagonal bores and optic sights; these enabled marksmen to record hits at up to 1,000 yards.

At the time of the Spanish-American War and World War I the bolt-action rifles issued as standard were of such high quality that gifted marksmen could 'make remarkable practice' simply by using telescope sights and hand-selected ammunition with the issue weapon. During World War II and since, most American infantrymen have carried semi- or fully-automatic weapons. Mass armies of conscripts, many of them from urban backgrounds and with only a few months' training, needed the means of delivering a lot of firepower. This stress on rapid fire at short battle ranges has persisted in weapons design and tactical doctrine, so the sniper has once more become a breed apart, with special skills and equipment.

Today's Green Berets, Navy SEALs, Marine Surveillance & Target Acquisition platoons, and snipers from many other units learn their craft at the Target Interdiction Course conducted by the Weapons Committee at Fort Bragg's Special Warfare Center. This extremely demanding programme teaches far more than just long-range precision shooting.

Students must learn to camouflage themselves perfectly, yet without compromising their ability to observe and to operate their equipment. They must learn to move invisibly across terrain - often with glacial slowness, perhaps only 100 yards in a day - while getting into a carefully selected position. They must learn how to build a 'hide' that is indetectible to someone standing directly on it; and to lie patiently inside it, with only chiggers, snakes and their own grumbling bladders for company, while the instructors roam the area searching for them. They must learn to make first-shot kills on targets at extreme ranges, under extreme conditions.

(**Above**) This team have just 'flopped' where they stood; even so, at any distance they would make indistinct targets. The weapon here is the .50cal RAI M500 sniper rifle with 10x scope; it has a muzzle brake/flash hider and a harmonic balancer, which damps down harmonic vibrations in the long, 'free-floating' barrel.

(**Opposite top**) The sniper with the M500 is backed by a spotter armed with a 7.62mm M21 - an accurized version of the old M14 - with 3-9x power adjustable scope. This was the Army's standard sniper rifle until the end of the 1980s.

(**Right**) Sniper/observer teams carry sophisticated optical equipment, including even laser target designators. This AN/PAS passive infrared viewer allows detection of men and equipment by their thermal signatures, without revealing the observer.

(**Far right**) The image seen through a night vision device - note the centred white dot.

In Vietnam some units used .50cal M2 machine guns for single-shot sniping with surprising success. Although not normally considered a precision weapon, the M2's heavy barrel and powerful cartridge combined to make an excellent – although rather immobile – sniper rifle. When the standard 'iron' sights were augmented with a high-magnification, low-light scope the M2 was deadly to ranges far beyond that of the M16. In scenarios such as the siege of Khe Sanh, characterised by long-term fighting from static positions, NVA soldiers were hit at distances of 1,000m and more.

In recent years the Army and Marines have shown interest in 'Special Application Rifles' designed around the .50cal (12.7mm) Browning machine gun cartridge, and a number of designs - e.g. by Barrett, Research Armament Industries (American Military Arms Corp.), and Iver Johnson - have been purchased for trials and issue to selected units, including the Special Forces. Innovations in buffering and recoil management make it practical to fire the .50cal round without reducing the shoulder to hamburger - often the case with various World War I and II experiments with large calibre anti-tank rifles. (The RAI M500 has a kick described as comparable to the shove of a 10-gauge shotgun; the Barrett M82A1 has a recoil of only 25.9 foot-pounds.)

These SARs are used for bringing precise, highly penetrative fire on 'high value' individuals, often behind cover - e.g. an enemy sniper behind a brick wall, or a commander in a lightly armoured vehicle. They can also make scrap out of the delicate parts of radar and commo equipment and parked aircraft, wreck the engines of vehicles, and detonate ordnance at a safe distance in the EOD role.

The M500 - mostly used by the Navy and Marines, but taken into action by SF in the Gulf - is an unconventional design, being a single-shot rifle whose bolt is removed after each shot, bringing the spent case with it. It is highly accurate and effective to 1,000m plus, but even though a sniper's work is necessarily deliberate the slow reloading is a drawback. As a result most SOCOM sniper teams are today equipped with the Barrett M82A1, a semi-automatic design with a 10-round box magazine. It has already proved lethally efficient on several battlefields. In the Gulf an Iraqi YW531 (BMP) APC was knocked out with two AP incendiary rounds at 1,100 meters. In Mogadishu, Somalia, in January 1993 five USMC snipers hit 15 of 'General' Adid's tank crewmen and ZSU-23-4 gunners at 600 yards, preventing a single man from entering their M48s or getting off a round from the quad-AAA mount.

(Above) M24 Remington 7.62mm sniper rifle fitted with PVS4 'starlight' scope - a passive image intensifier which enhances available natural light. The M24 system was replacing the M21 as the standard equipment at about the time of the Gulf War. Its normal daytime sight is a 10x M3A scope; and the accompanying observer usually carries a 20x M49 spotter scope.

(Opposite top & centre) The M82A1 Barrett 'Light Fifty', with (top) a comparison between its round and the standard 5.56mm M16 cartridge. The graticule of the Leupold & Stevens M3A Ultra 10x scope is adjustable for various ammunition types (e.g. armour-piercing incendiary) at ranges between 500 and 1,800 metres.

(Right) Observer with AN/PAS7 IR viewer, and sniper using a PVS4 starlight scope. They are exposed deliberately for the camera - in real life they would never silhouette themselves against the background like this.

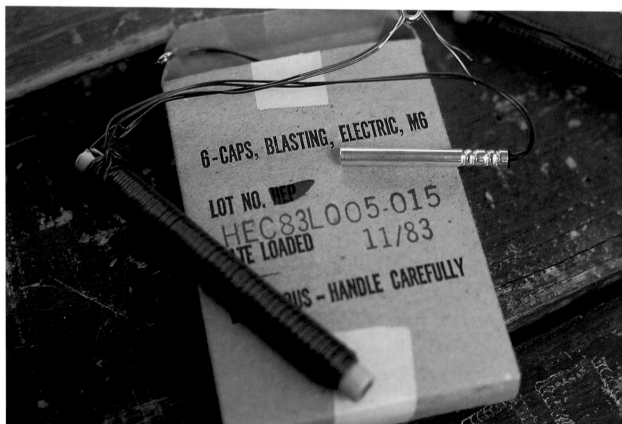

CHARGE, DEMOLITION, BLOCK, M5A1

Anti-personnel grenades are like knives – something to use when the enemy is very close and you have few choices. SF soldiers carry them, sometimes in large numbers, but try hard to avoid situations where frag grenades have to be used. The current standard issue is the M67 (**opposite top**), about the size of a baseball. This can be thrown out to 40m and has a delay time of between four and five seconds. It is filled with Composition B explosive; when it explodes its fragmentation casualty radius is rated at 15m,

but the effects of grenades are notoriously unpredictable, both for better and for worse.

Many other kinds of US and foreign fragmentation, concussion and incendiary grenades are issued to SF units; one is the small M560 series, designed for clearing rooms without clearing the assault team at the same time. Smoke grenades have always been another staple item for patrol members; the standard M18, about the size of a beer can, is normally used to signal aircraft, both for pick-ups and to

indicate position when calling in tactical air support. M18s are available in green, red, white, purple, and yellow, the choice of the correct identifying colour sometimes being of life-or-death importance - the enemy has smoke grenades, too, and may attempt to lure in or misdirect your aircraft.

'One thing wrong with training today is that a lot of guys have never actually drawn grenades and jumped with them – things change significantly when you can detonate yourself. And they're heavy, too. But if

there's one essential lesson to pass along to today's troops, it is: Don't play with grenades! I don't know what the fascination is, but people insist on messing with grenades, with unfortunate consequences. You don't need to modify the flare on the cotter key to make it easier to pull the ring – that's for the movies! You can spray paint them black, and wear them low on your vest or LBE, to make it harder for the enemy to see them and to shoot at them. But don't play with them.'
(SSGT Buck Ravenscroft)

(**Opposite**) Electrical blasting caps.

(**Above**) C4 plastic explosive, a substance with a hundred applications in SF operations.

(**Right**) Military explosives: dynamite, detonating cord, blasting caps, TNT, fuse, and fuse lighter.

(**Above**) The old ones are sometimes still the good ones: like the rest of the armed forces, SF still employ large numbers of M18A1 Claymore anti-personnel mines - this one identified by its blue colour as a practice round. The fibre-glass case holds 1.5lbs of C4, fronted by a layer of 700 steel ball bearings. The Claymore is either command-detonated with an electrical initiator at the end of 30m of wire, or can be rigged to detonate when a tripwire is disturbed. When it goes off the mine blows its ball bearings forward in a horizontal fan pattern which is lethal out to 25 metres.

(**Left**) The M57 firing device, used to initiate Claymore mines.

Uniforms: The Green Beret

The story of the origin of the green beret as the US Army Special Forces' distinctive headgear has several variations. It certainly dates from the early 1950s as an nauthorized item. One version claims that the first ones were ought in a Fayetteville, North Carolina, ladies' millinery shop y a couple of young sergeants. Participating in war games with he 82nd Airborne Division in the role of guerrilla fighters, they vanted to look the part. Coloured berets were associated since World War II with elite units of the British and other European rmies, and these sergeants thought they would look appropriate.

Another version credits Major Hubert Bruckner and 1st Lt. Roger Pezelle with the original introduction, in 1953, as nofficial headgear for Pezelle's A-team, FA-32 of 10th SFGA. ezelle's team wore the beret whenever they went to the field in Germany, and the idea caught on with 77th SFGA back at t.Bragg. Soon all SF troopers in the field were wearing this ighly illegal, privately acquired green beret.

Now, the beret would not have become a big deal, and oday's Special Forces would wear the same kind of hats as the est of the Army, had those little teams of SF role-playing uerrillas not regularly created havoc among the 82nd in the war ames. Often infiltrating heavily guarded command posts to 'kill' ey personnel or detonate simulated explosives, they were not ticking to the script. The 82nd's commander became very upset vith these unconventional troops. As a veteran of that old Army he author can assure readers that things were *very* different back n the late 1950s and early '60s. There are few on active duty oday who can recall the years of spit-shined boots and heavily ailored and starched fatigues. The 82nd was a command where tarch and shine were very important. The SF teams from Smoke Bomb Hill didn't worry much about all that, and sometimes wore eans in the field, along with those ridiculous berets. There was omething gleeful about their successful exploits that just drove he Army nuts. In 1956 the 82nd (and Ft.Bragg post) commander ecreed that wearing a beret, in the field or back in garrison, was court-martial offence.

The berets went into hiding in the USA, although they ontinued to be worn on a local basis in Germany. In September 961 Brig.Gen.William Yarborough, commandant of the Special Varfare Center, used his connections with a military aide to President John F.Kennedy to finally get the green beret approved; vhen JFK visited Ft.Bragg to review the SF the following month e was highly impressed, and commented favourably on what he aw - including the beret. The visit produced a tremendous amount f positive press attention, and suddenly the Green Berets were America's most elite soldiers. The beret became a symbol, in and ut of the Army, for a different way of doing business. Forty years ater it remains the emblem of a particularly skillful soldier who as been trained and tested to a particularly high standard.

PFC Lonnie Holmes wearing his Class A uniform in the mid-1960s, after completing the Q-Course but before assignment to Vietnam. He wears the SF crest directly on the beret and on his epaulettes. Under the AIRBORNE tab is the SF shoulder patch adopted in 1955 - a teal blue arrowhead shape (recalling the red arrowhead of the World War II 1st Special Service Force), with a gold shortsword crossed by three gold lightning bolts. The shined black 'Corcorans' are a prized sign of the SF's airborne status. Lonnie's jump wings are worn on the teal blue and yellow background oval first worn by the 77th SFGA. (Photo Lonnie Holmes)

Some within the SF community deeply resent being called 'Green Berets'; they will tell you that it is only a hat, and that the 1960s media hype, the maudlin Barry Saddler song, the Rambo movies, and many similar fictions have misrepresented their demanding profession. They insist on being called Special Forces soldiers, and would rather be seen as what they call 'quiet professionals'.

Apart from the special-to-arm headgear and insignia, SF have nearly always worn the same uniforms as other US airborne infantry. In the 1950s this meant the M1951/53 field uniform in Olive Green 107 and, in garrison, the Army Green Class A uniform or Army Khaki in summer. In 1963 SF were the first to receive the Tropical Combat Uniform, the lightweight 'jungle fatigues'. Several patterns of OG 107 utilities continued to be worn alongside the three evolving patterns of jungle fatigues. In Vietnam in the early 1960s some advisors wore spotted 'duck-hunter' camouflage from commercial or local sources; and by the mid-1960s various 'tigerstripe' patterns were commonly seen when in the field. The first US general issue camouflage clothing, the ERDL pattern, appeared in the late 1960s. The Battle Dress Uniform was first issued in both temperate and desert camouflage patterns in 1982.

(Left) Warrant Officer 2 wearing his rank insignia (note silver bar with two black lines) through the red flash identifying the 7th SFGA, on his 'rifle green' beret. (Photo William B. Folsom)

(Above) SFC Jamie Allen, 12th SFGA, in OG jungle fatigues with dull metal collar rank insignia and jump wings. The bear is a qualified parachutist, but does not go on ops.

(Left) US Army parachutist's wings, for which all SF soldiers must qualify. On Class A uniform they are worn on oval cloth backgrounds in teal blue and yellow or specific unit colours.

(Below left) The beret flash, in Group or other unit identifying colours, was introduced with the beret in 1961; this example identified the 6th SFGA. Officers and WOs wear their rank insignia, enlisted ranks the Special Forces branch insignia as here.

(Above) The Army Green uniform worn by two SF veterans: left, Command Sergeant Major Russell Mann, and right, commanding officer Lieutenant-Colonel Gerry Schumacher of 3rd Bn., 12th SFGA. Green 'leadership' loops, with the branch insignia, are worn by officers and NCOs in the direct line of unit command. Officers and WOs wear rank insignia on the epaulettes, NCOs on the sleeves. Officers wear the SF

crossed arrows on the lower lapel below the national ciphers; enlisted men wear one 'US' and one branch insignia on collar discs. US personal decorations and qualifications are worn on the left breast, foreign and collective unit citations on the right.

Russ Mann wears the Combat Medical Badge above his rows of medal ribbons, which include the Army Commendation Medal with three clusters, and are headed by the Bronze Star with V for Valour. Below the ribbons are his jump wings, and the silver 'bubblehead' badge of a qualified SF SCUBA diver. Among the insignia on his right breast are Canadian jump wings, the Vietnamese Cross of Gallantry, and the Vietnamese Civic Action award with palm. The full colour Special Forces shoulder patch with AIRBORNE and 1983 SPECIAL FORCES tabs are displayed by LTC Schumacher. Just hinted at on Mann's left forearm is the elbow-high stack of 'hash marks' showing his many years of service.

(Above) Some of the medals won by Special Forces soldiers in Vietnam and elsewhere: the Medal of Honor, Legion of Merit, Silver Star, Distinguished Flying Cross, Bronze Star, Air Medal and Purple Heart. In addition to the 17 Medals of Honor awarded to Green Berets in South-East Asia in the 1950s-1970s, 105 received the Distinguished Service Cross; 902 received the Silver Star; and 13,234 were awarded the Bronze Star with V. Those totals are misleading, however, as most SF units required a much higher standard for awards than conventional units; a Bronze Star with V on the uniform of a Green Beret is the equivalent to a Silver Star on somebody in a conventional unit. Awards of the apparently anachronistic Distinguished Flying Cross and Air Medal were not uncommon; SF personnel spent a lot of time aloft in helicopters and light reconnaissance aircraft, and often came under fire in the air.

(Left) Subdued field versions of the SF shoulder patch, AIRBORNE and SPECIAL FORCES tabs.

(Opposite top) A-Detachment from 7th SFGA. They wear lightweight BDUs, as introduced from 1985, with load-bearing equipment based on the ALICE system. SF soldiers spend a lot of time setting up their LBE, which carries at least two ammunition pouches, two water canteens, grenades, wound dressing (always on the upper left suspender), knife, and generally strobe light to signal extraction helicopters. The individual components of the harness are chosen based on team SOP and the whims of the individual.

(Opposite bottom) Lightweight BDUs and patrol cap. The red bracelet on the right wrist is interesting; some US soldiers and Marines wear one marked with the name and date of disappearance of a Vietnam 'MIA' - a soldier missing in action.

(Top) Since Vietnam the 'boonie hat', issued or modified in various versions, has been the favoured field headgear. The reflective 'cat's-eye' patches stuck to the back make it easier to locate the other members of a team during night operations.

(Above centre & above) Despite the parallel capabilities of the Navy SEALs, SF groups maintain some SCUBA-trained A-Teams, largely for insertion by water into enemy-held areas, although various underwater reconnaissance and recovery skills are also taught at the Key West SCUBA school. Here SGT David Wein of Co.A, 2nd Bn., 7th SFGA, emerges from the water wearing BDUs over his wetsuit. The LAR V Draeger 'rebreather' unit captures and recycles exhaled air, thus preventing any tell-tale bubbles on the surface. (Photos William B. Folsom)

(Above) The 'Fritz' - officially, Personal Armor System for Ground Troops (PASGT) helmet - is standard issue to Special Forces, as to all other US Army infantry. Like all helmets, it is unpopular on account of its weight, and in the field is sometimes carried slung until necessary - 'an airburst is God's way of telling you to put it on'. This captain displays dull metal rank bars on his helmet cover; note also, on his right and left collars respectively, subdued rank bars and Special Forces crossed arrows. (Photo William B Folsom)

(Opposite) SGT David Wein demonstrates infiltration techniques. His wetsuit is still worn beneath his BDUs and basic ALICE equipment. (Photo William B. Folsom)

Opposite) SGT Wein scouting forward through the swamp. His basic ALICE belt, suspenders, pouches and canteens are supplemented with various other personally acquired pouches.

Below) Special Forces commo man using his 'leg key' to send a Morse transmission, reading from his encryption pad.

Modern radio direction finding equipment can determine the position of a transmitter if the operator stays on the air for more than a few moments. SF tactical communications therefore rely on 'burst' systems which transmit messages almost instantly, before an enemy RDF can lock on to the signal. Burst messages are sent through a Digital Message Device Group (DMDG), a small keyboard terminal which encrypts a typed message and packages it for transmission through a satellite radio or through a conventional PRC-70 or -74.

'The DMDG allows the unit to send a message one of several ways', explains former SF captain and commo officer David Wemhoff. 'One involves encryption with a built-in electronic key. Another uses a "commo card" issued by the communications section of the unit. That lets you sit back in some safe location, type up the message at your leisure, check it over, then send correct, secure, current "Intel" back to the people who need it.'

SF units inserted in hostile territory normally communicate on a pre-set schedule. Most of the time the radio is turned off; the team has communications 'windows' when routine messages are scheduled for transmission, and when messages for the team are routinely received. Windows will vary, based partially on available frequencies, on satellites overhead, the area of operations, sunspot activity, and other factors.

(Above) The SF soldier - and anybody else who spends serious time in the field - does not rely on the standard slide fasteners which attach the components of the ALICE system. He uses parachute suspension line (a.k.a.'dummy cord') and/or '100mph tape' to secure canteens, mag pouches, holsters, and anything else to the web gear - otherwise it invariably falls off at the worst possible moment.

In Vietnam in 1968 Special Forces developed the STABO extraction harness; this combined load-carrying equipment with a strong shoulder and leg harness resembling a parachute rig. If extraction helicopters could not land, they dropped 147- foot ropes with strong webbing bridles. The team attached these to D-rings and carabiners on the STABO harness, and up to four men could be plucked up and away by each Huey. They could not be winched up into the helicopter, and the ride to safety was notoriously uncomfortable - but better than being left to fight it out with a horde of NVA.

(Centre left) The standard issue patrol compass, a basic tool for any SF soldier - and one that gets a tremendous work-out during the land navigation phase of the Q-Course. The basic skills of navigation by map and compass must never be allowed to degrade, despite the extraordinary facility offered by the Global Positioning System - as soon as you start to rely on it, Sod's Law dictates that the battery will run down.

(Below left) The strobe light was designed to help downed aircrew signal to rescuers, but has been adopted by SF soldiers for night signalling to helicopters when it is time for extraction. It emits a bright blue flashing light, and on a clear night can be seen up to 10 miles away.

(Left) LBE vests like this example are used on an *ad hoc* basis by all SOCOM units. The exact configuration depends on the unit's SOP and the particular mission, which dictates what has to be carried.

(Below) The Magellan GPS 1000 receiver, one of several types in use by SF; it gave good service during the Gulf War.

The Global Positioning System is based on 24 navigation satellites in Earth orbit. Receivers need to pick up the signals from a minimum of four; these are collated and the information is converted into usable data, e.g. the receiver's latitude and longitude and height above sea level - other data is available depending on the way the specific receiver is set up. By use of the military 'P-code' which overrides the 'Coarse Acquisition' error deliberately built into the GPS system by the Department of Defense, an accuracy of 10m (33 feet) is achievable.

This capability - to find out exactly where you are on the surface of the planet, to within a stone's throw, by night or day and in all weathers - would have seemed like science fiction, or an impossible miracle, to soldiers of previous generations. Like all miracles, however, it sometimes fails to happen. It is not a foregone conclusion that the right combination of satellites are going to be over your head when you need them; and if you don't have a sustainable external power source (i.e. if you are on clandestine operations, on foot, in rough terrain - as SF soldiers tend to be) then the batteries have a limited life.

During the Vietnam War SF soldiers experimented with various load-carrying vests to replace their conventional LBE based on a waist belt and shoulder suspenders. A fabric vest with many integral pockets of various sizes would offer better weight distribution, and a more versatile stowage of a variety of munitions, survival and signalling kit, than separate pouches arranged on belt and suspenders. Climatic conditions are limiting factors; in the tropics constant pressure and chafing over a large area of sweat-soaked shirt is a recipe for instant skin disorders.

In Vietnam the USAF pilot's SRU-21/P vest was popular, its body being made of open netting. SF also designed special vests for rifleman, machine gunner and medic, but they were turned down by the Army. Over the years SF have used various improvised or modified rigs, e.g. based on the 40mm grenadier's ammo vest or on police designs.

In 1988 the US Army made the first issue to trials units - including Special Forces - of the Individual Tactical Load-Bearing Vest (ITLBV) as part of the Integrated Individual Fighting System (IIFS) designed to replace the ALICE gear in infantry units. The ITLBV is a three-part lace-together Kevlar vest (with minimal splinter protection - it is worn over the PASGT body armour) with broad, padded suspenders. It incorporates six magazine and two grenade pouches, and attaches to the ALICE belt, which supports the canteens, E-tool, and other necessities. A pack system attaches to the back.

Load-bearing vests are suitable for some missions, but not for others. One fundamental of SF operations is that rapid evasion may sometimes require the rucksack to be dropped, leaving soldiers to survive with what they have in their 'belt order' only. Distributing vital items in the various parts of a belt-and-vest rig would take careful thought.

(Left) The PRC-70 is still sometimes used for patrol communication, although seldom for voice communications. The PRC-70 doesn't have a lot of power, but if the 'long wire' antenna has been rigged properly you can have commo links with your company or battalion radio operator hundreds of miles away.

(Below) 12th SFGA commo team using a PRC-70 HF radio to talk to another team 500 miles away.

(Opposite top) SCR-100 satellite link radio with antenna; this allows clear, reasonably secure voice communications around the world.

(Opposite bottom) SF teams sometimes use short-range squad radios like this URC-68, but their range is too limited for most operations.

The workhorse radio for SF units has been the PRC-74, operating between 2 and 12 Megahertz (Mz). If only batteries are available it can operate on 10 to 12 volts, and the battery pack gives about 24 hours of continuous operation. Like the older PRC-70, the 74 can be hooked up to a vehicle's electrical system, which really bumps up its output. The wattage is not very high, but since transmissions are normally 'sky-bursts' rather than ground wave the signal can be bounced off the stratosphere toward a receiver many miles away. This requires the assembly of a long wire antenna tuned to the specific frequency.

Although SF radio men still learn code and the intricacies of the PRC-74, today they typically use satellite technology. Systems like the SRC-100 allow an A-Detachment to chat with anybody, anywhere on the globe, clearly and reliably. These 'satcom' radios are simple and compact. The antenna unfolds and is pointed toward a section

of the sky where one of the DoD satellites is known to be; the operator just has to dial in a pair of pre-assigned frequencies.

There are two downsides to this technological marvel. One is the need to pre-schedule the frequencies used: there is a lot of competition for the available channels, and not enough to go around.

The other is that if you can talk to anybody, then they can talk to you. That means that the President, the Secretary of Defense, or somebody back in the Pentagon can call up a team deep in enemy territory with helpful hints, suggestions, and requests. These are seldom appreciated. In the past the team's PRC-70 could suddenly and mysteriously 'malfunction' at such moments, but satcom systems make that less credible. SF operators tend to be adamant on the topic: this radio is good for sending out situation reports and calls for support while a team is deployed, but bad when it is used to 'micromanage' an operation.

Parachutes

SSGT Buck Ravenscroft, on SF parachuting:

'I made my first military jump in 1961, back when we were using the old T-10, an improved version of the T-7 used during World War II. Then we discovered that civilian skydivers were using canopies with double-L and T/U modifications, followed by the Para-Commander... Special Forces strongly lusted after such things! The chances of our getting [them] in the early 60s seemed very slim - until we found that the SEAL teams were using double-L canopies. We said, "If those Navy guys can use manoeuverable canopies, we sure as hell can, too!" The result was the MC1, the grandmother of all Army manoeuverable canopies.

'While some guys had problems with it, particularly when they pulled the toggle pin all the way down and went corkscrewing into the ground, I never had trouble with it. Now you had some forward velocity – you could steer into the wind to land, and you could steer toward your team rally point on the DZ. Then came an improved version with better steering control and an anti-inversion net at the skirt of the canopy, [which] eliminated the "Mae West" inversion that used to be such a common problem. Then we got the MC1-1 canopy and a much improved harness.

'It used to be a real test of strength for you and your buddies to get a Special Forces-sized ruck attached to the old-sized D-ring on the harness. We did that for 10 or 12 years before the introduction of the single-point release, a big improvement. When I first started in SF we didn't use lowering lines; we rode our rucks to the ground. Then, sometime in the 1970s, we started using lowering lines. What a zoo that was!

'Each of us made our own, usually from climbing ropes. Somebody would deploy a ruck ... and it would come screaming past you like a shot. The opening shock of the canopy was nothing compared to the shock of a heavy ruck dropping to the end of a 50-foot line! Some guys attached the line to their leg straps, but you only did that once!

'An SF soldier works in the sky. That is one of the ways we get to work. While you're under the canopy you need to be alert and observant of what's happening in the air around you and on the ground ... We're as busy during descent as we are in the aircraft ... We have a plan, and we execute it even before we hit the ground.

'And we don't go to work on a bright, clear Sunday afternoon - you're going on a Tuesday night, in the middle of a storm, when it is dark and rainy, because that's when you'll have the best chance for survival and mission accomplishment. That's why we attend Rough-Terrain Parachute School, spending days and nights doing nothing but jumping into trees ... .

'I think most SF operators think parachuting is a crucial part of their role ... It takes tremendous discipline. And it all culminates, eventually, in the back of a C-130 or -141 in the middle of the night, one minute before you give the jump command, when everybody is hooked up and standing in the door, waiting for the green light ... The airplane is turning, and all you can see out the door is a big black hole. If you're the jumpmaster, that's when you look each man square in the eye and there's an unspoken comm-unication between you of mutual trust and respect. It sounds funny now, but it wasn't funny then – I thought to myself that it was a tremendous honor to be on a team of such men, on such missions.'

(Opposite top) SGTs Ravens-croft and Cardin are older than most of the men on their team, but wiser, too ... Here they wear MC1-1B steerable chutes with T-10 reserves.

(Opposite bottom) Some individuals qualify for HALO (High Altitude exit, Low altitude Opening) and HAHO (High Altitude, High Opening), for almost indetectible insertion. Both are typically done by night, from above 20,000 feet, with sophisticated rigs like this MT1-XX ram-air chute. HALO jumpers fall to 2,500 feet or less before opening their chutes; HAHO jumpers open theirs almost immediately, then glide long distances before landing. Both require insulated overalls, protective 'bunny' helmet and goggles, and oxygen.

(Right) 12th SFGA jumpers in the '80s - in old M1C steel helmets and OG jungle fatigues - prepare to stand up and hook up before leaving a DH Caribou.

(Below) SFC Jamie Allen shouts 'Stand in the door!'

(Right) Jumping from a C-130, this soldier's canopy is just about to open. Although World War II-style massed airdrops are a thing of the past, SF soldiers have to maintain proficiency with a jump at least every three months. Parachuting is perfect for the kind of clandestine insertions that might someday be required of them.

(Below left) Practice jump with 'plain vanilla' T-10 canopy, and rucksack deployed on its 16-foot quick-release line. The T-10 is steerable to some extent by hauling down on one of the risers, to tilt the canopy and spill some air, letting you make a turn or a slip.

(Below right) 'Hollywood' jump - i.e. without combat equipment - with the MC1-1B canopy. This has forward speed and is truly steerable, with lines controlling the flow of air through the missing gores to pivot the canopy away from hazards.

Sergeant Major Russ Mann, SF Medic

You would think there was a standard issue kit for the gear you'd take on patrol, but that's not the way it worked in Vietnam. As a medic, I was issued an empty M5 bag that could be carried with its own straps or attached to a harness or ruck. We tailored the contents of the bag, depending on the mission.

'For most of us, that included a standard set of surgical tools – forceps, scalpels, haemostats, scissors, and needle-holders. We added to that whatever we thought we'd need for the patrol. We went over to Medical Supply and walked down the rows collecting items: battle dressings, triangular dressings, all kinds of compresses, airways, IV solutions, and safety pins. Now, safety pins are great for a combat medic – you can temporarily close a wound with them, for example; and if you're having trouble maintaining an unconscious soldier's airway, you can just use a safety pin to hold his tongue to his lip. You can use them to remove splinters, and all sorts of other things. Safety pins are wonderful!

'We also used a lot of Foley catheters, a device normally used to drain the bladder. But in a pinch, they make great chest tubes when you're dealing with a sucking chest wound. You can use them for tourniquets, and they make fine slingshots, too.

'We made our own airways out of plastic syringe barrels, and I carried a couple of these in my pocket. When someone can't breathe through their nose or mouth, you make a hole in their trachea and insert one of these. I spent a lot of my combat time at Khe Sanh, where we were engaged in trench warfare; most of the wounds were in the head and face. I worked on a lot of airway problems – where somebody's face is folded into their throat, they don't breathe very well!

'We could do a lot of surgery, and did tons of minor wound repair from shrapnel, knives, and bullets. We didn't ship anybody out unless they really needed true surgical intervention.

'Every team had an SOP [Standard Operating Procedures] just for what you carried and where it went on your harness. Your 'blow-out patch' - a wound dressing suitable for sucking chest wounds - always went on the upper portion of your left harness. That way, if your buddy was wounded in combat you used his dressing and you knew right where to find it. If he was dead, and you needed his ammo, you knew where to find that, too.

'In addition to my specialized gear, here's what I carried on patrol:

'A government-issue Boy Scout knife with a screwdriver, a can-opener and a blade. (This was before Leatherman knives were available – today everybody has one). The knife was great for opening C-ration cans and slicing salami.

'We wore jungle boots (no socks), and tigerstripe fatigues without underwear - underwear traps moisture and causes rashes in the jungle. My compass was in my shirt pocket, along with cigarettes and lighter. The cigarettes were useful for removing leeches. Most of us carried some sort of hide-out gun in one of the pockets. Mine was a tiny Colt snub-nose .38 revolver.

'I had two smoke grenades permanently taped to the harness; these were of different colors and were used to signal the extraction helicopter during emergencies. I had a strobe light, too, for emergency signalling, in a pouch on the harness. A couple of additional smoke grenades for routine marking of

DZs were also carried on the harness, along with my combat knife, a Model 2 Randall. This was a big survival knife.

'I usually carried two quarts of water in canteens on my belt, and then we used canteen covers for everything else on the belt. Nobody used the issued magazine pouches; they only held three mags. You can get seven 20-round magazines in a canteen cover – five vertically and two on top. I carried two of those – 14 magazines are a LOT of rounds!

'Another pouch – I don't remember what kind or where it came from – was for hand grenades, and held eight or ten.

'A signal mirror and a couple of recognition panels got stowed on the harness, too, in an improvised case of some sort. This case might also include Band-Aids and water purification tablets.

'You had to have a caribiner, gloves, and a short length of rope you could tie into a Swiss seat for helicopter extraction from deep jungle. At this point, the harness is getting heavy! The harness never comes off during the entire time you're on patrol.

'In addition, we often carried a rucksack. Inside were normally a poncho and poncho liner, and everybody carried a couple of mortar rounds or belts of machine gun ammunition for

the crew-served weapon used on the patrol. You would probably carry a LAW, the little Light Antitank Weapon used against enemy bunkers; a handful of 'toe-popper' mines, and maybe a couple of Claymore mines. The toe-poppers were great – about the size and shape of a can of Sterno, made of green plastic, with a dial on top to set the mine. It just took a second to stop and place one of these if you were running up a trail with a bunch of bad guys after you. That would slow them down a little. One or two 2-quart canteens full of water also went into the ruck.

Each of us normally carried a roll of "det" [detonating] cord, some blasting caps, and a block of C4.

'If things got bad, you could abandon the rucksack and run, and still have the minimal items necessary for survival.'

Weapons

'Most of the time I used a CAR-15 for my personal weapon – it was more compact than the M16, effective out to 100 meters or so. I carried other weapons, including the BAR [Browning Automatic Rifle], shotguns, M16s, and the Swedish K. The BAR was one of the great weapons of the world – heavy, but highly effective, and would cut down small trees!

'The Spike Teams, the spooky guys that ran the cross-border operations, usually carried CAR-15s, but the Mike Forces and Hatchet Forces – the rapid reaction forces made up mostly of Montagnards led by Special Forces guys – used weapons that were more haphazard. The one I was attached to used Swedish Ks almost exclusively; it seemed to depend on what was

available at the time. I've seen some equipped with World War ⅠⅠ weapons - M3 .45cal 'grease guns', [Browning M1919] A machine guns - and most of them worked great.

'There were certainly lots of SF guys who preferred AK: who thought it was a superior weapon; it certainly was mor reliable. But personally I wasn't impressed with its accuracy. was more comfortable with the M16 or the CAR-15. The M16 a hell of an accurate rifle. I only had one jam, and that wasn't i combat. The CAR-15's maximum practical effective range wa only about 100 to 150 meters, but that was because of the sigl radius, which was much shorter than the standard M16. But man-sized target at 150 meters is not a problem with the weapor which is more than you can say for any of the 9mm weapons lik the Swedish K. Remember, you don't have to kill the guy for th shot to be effective – it is okay to wound him, and sometime better, because it takes two guys out of combat, the wounded ma. and his buddy who attends to him.'

Knives

'One very common blade carried by SF guys on patrol was th little sheath knife issued to Air Force crews. It has a serrate back that can be used to saw through small trees, and a smal sharpening stone in a pouch attached to the sheath. A lot of guy liked that for its size. A lot of other guys carried Ka-Bars. Th rest tended to carry Randall or Gerber combat knives.

'In general, people tended to carry a lot more knife tha they needed or intended to use. You used your knife to open C ration cans, or to cut down small trees - no, actually, we used de cord to cut down small trees. The big knives were generall useless, and you used the small folding knife in your pocket mos of the time. The big knives were a last resort, and if you neede it for something important, you were in trouble! Everybod thinks Special Forces guys are all knife-fighting experts, traine to slit the throats of sentries in the dark. But I think we got a tota of one hour's instruction on where to stab people, and the subjec was never again mentioned.

Patrol Rations

'You could eat anything you wanted on patrol, and that usuall meant either C-rations or "indig" rations. Most of the time w took the Cs, but sometimes replaced them with the indigenou meals. The indig rations were lighter, and provided some novelty Even people who hated Chinese food in the States would get s tired of the Cs that they'd go for the indigenous version for change of taste. These were manufactured on Okinawa, unde the direction of the legendary Ben Baker, and were designed t please the tastes of the tribesmen in the highlands. The meal were basically rice with either dried shrimp or pork and othe ingredients, plus a small packet of pepper you could mix in t suit your personal "compression ratio".

Tools of the Trade Today

'Things haven't fundamentally changed much since then. We stil carry the M16 and CAR-15, now called the M4. Night visio goggles, laser-designators, and GPS have been the majo improvements. But the personal equipment that the soldie carries on his body is still the same set of stuff. The M16 – nov in the US inventory for over 40 years – will continue to be issue for the foreseeable future. No replacement has been mentioned.